The May~~flower~~ House

Terri Rohde

Photography: Tracy Watts

Dedication

To all the spirits of the May Stringer House, without your presence and communication with us this would not have been possible.

Four more steps to the top, an open doorway awaits you.

You step inside.

The thickness of the air surrounds you.

Are you being watched?

Uneasiness fills the air.

A dark shadow drifts from a room down the hall.

A sad cry of a child yearning for her mother can be heard in the distance.

Look through your camera lens, you may see a darting ball of light. Is it just the dust from an old attic? Or could these be orbs of spirit energy?

The two story Queen Anne style home that overlooks the city of Brooksville was built in 1865 by John May. The original home had four rooms.

The home was eventually bought by Dr. Sheldon Stringer, who practiced medicine there. He enlarged the house to its current size of 14 rooms.

Dr. Stringer later treated patients with diseases of the times such as small pox and yellow fever in his office which was located on the first floor of the home.

In the 19th Century it was a common practice to photograph the dead. Photographs were very expensive and a death photograph was often the last memory a family had of their loved one.

The most famous spirit said to reside at the May Stringer is but a child. Jessie May died in the home at the age of three.

Jessie May is a playful spirit, often moving her toys and hiding museum artifacts under her bed.

Paranormal investigators have reported hearing sounds of crying and an extra voice chanting along to 'Itsy Bitsy Spider'. Could Jessie be reaching out?

When an old trunk was donated to the museum and placed in the attic, many say the atmosphere in the attic changed. One docent at the museum refuses to enter the attic, even on tours.

The docent claims she has had more than one negative encounter with the new attic resident. In one incident she even reported being pushed. Does the spirit in the attic want to be left alone?

The docent refers to the male spirit in the attic as "Mr. Nasty".
A psychic believes his name may be Gary and that in life he worked as an actor in the vaudeville theatre.

Paranormal investigators have captured many recorded EVP's (Electronic Voice Phenomenon) believed to belong to the spirits of Gary or Jessie.

REM-pod

EDI Meter

K2 Meter

Voice recorder for EVPs.

Pictures taken in the home are often riddled with mists, balls or ropes of unexplained light or eerie shadows.

Most visitors to the museum today come simply to step back in time and appreciate one of Brooksville's original homes.

Along with the attic,
master bedroom,
children's room, parlor,
dining room, kitchen and
doctor's office, the
museum also houses
some special rooms.

A communication room houses a 1926 telephone switchboard and other communication devices from the early 1900's.

One room is designated "The Military Room". It is a make shift memorial to all those who serve our country. The walls are decorated with items donated by the families of servicemen in the community.

You may choose to visit the May Stringer House to view its magnificent Victorian architecture or revel in the simple feel of days gone by.

Or you may choose to visit hoping to capture a ghostly image on film or even a recorded voice from one of the home's former residents or spirit guests.

But whatever your reason for coming, your trip to the May Stringer House will leave a mark upon your soul that you will not soon forget.

The Hernando Heritage Museum, The May Stringer House, is open for tours Tuesday – Saturday from noon until 3pm.

They also offer ghost tours on Friday or Saturday nights by appointment.

Seasoned paranormal teams can even rent the home for a private late night investigation.

Are you ready to meet the spirits?

Glossary:

- **Orb** - Sphere or globe shaped spot, either white or colored that appear in photographs at presumed haunted locations
- **Victorian** - Refers to something characteristic of the period of the reign of Queen Victoria (1837 - 1901)
- **Artifact** - A handmade object or the remains of one from a particular historical period
- **Reside** - Live
- **Memorial** - Something designed to preserve the memory of a person or event
- **Paranormal** - Something that is outside of or beyond the normal, something that can not be explained

Web Links:

- http://www.hernandohistoricalmuseumassoc.com

- ghostsnghouls.com/2013/02/03/may-stringer-house-haunted/

- https://en.wikipedia.org/wiki/May-Stringer_House

- www.tampabay.com/...at...may-stringer.../1031563

- www.hauntedplaces.org/item/may-stringer-house/

- espexplorers.com

- facebook.com/esp.2009

About the Author

Terri Rohde resides in Bradenton, Florida where she works as a school librarian and a medical assistant. She obtained her Bachelor's degree in Education from USF and her Master's degree from Nova Southeastern University. She is the co-founder, case manager and lead investigator of ESP – Explorers of Spirit Phenomena, a paranormal research team founded in 2009. She's been attempting communication with the spirit world since she was a child and has always felt every connected to that world.

About the Photographer

Tracy Watts is a fifth generation Floridian currently living in Bradenton. She began her career teaching emotionally disturbed children and presently works as a library media specialist. She obtained her Bachelor's degree in Education and her Master's degree in Library & Information Science from USF. She is the production manager for the team, ESP – Explorers of Spirit Phenomena. Her first paranormal experience as a child occurred less than a mile from the team's home base.

Made in United States
Orlando, FL
15 April 2022

16880240R00020